I0813906

WHY DO BIRDS FLY SOUTH FOR WINTER?

by Debbie Vilardi

Cody Koala

An Imprint of Pop!
popbooksonline.com

abdobooks.com
Published by Pop!, a division of ABDO, PO Box 398166, Minneapolis, Minnesota 55439.

Printed in the United States of America, North Mankato, Minnesota

082018
012019

THIS BOOK CONTAINS RECYCLED MATERIALS

Cover Photo: iStockphoto
Interior Photos: iStockphoto, 1, 10, 13 (top), 13 (bottom right), 14; Shutterstock Images, 5 (top), 5 (bottom left), 5 (bottom right), 6, 9, 13 (bottom left), 19, 20; Red Line Editorial, 17

Editor: Meg Gaertner
Series Designer: Laura Mitchell

Library of Congress Control Number: 2018950121

Publisher's Cataloging-in-Publication Data
Names: Vilardi, Debbie, author.
Title: Why do birds fly south for winter? / by Debbie Vilardi.
Description: Minneapolis, Minnesota : Pop!, 2019 | Series: Science questions | Includes online resources and index.
Identifiers: ISBN 9781532162169 (lib. bdg.) | ISBN 9781641855877 (pbk) | ISBN 9781532163227 (ebook)
Subjects: LCSH: Birds--Behavior--Juvenile literature. | Birds--Migration--Juvenile literature. | Migration--Juvenile literature. | Children's questions and answers--Juvenile literature.
Classification: DDC 500--dc23

Hello! My name is

Cody Koala

Pop open this book and you'll find QR codes like this one, loaded with information, so you can learn even more!

Scan this code* and others like it while you read, or visit the website below to make this book pop.

popbooksonline.com/birds-fly-south

*Scanning QR codes requires a web-enabled smart device with a QR code reader app and a camera.

Table of Contents

Chapter 1

Birds

There are thousands of **species** of birds. At least 4,000 of them **migrate**. Birds in the United States fly south for winter. They return north for summer.

Watch a video here!

Some of these birds travel short distances. They move from one state to another. Others fly thousands of miles to their new homes.

Some birds fly for days without stopping.

Chapter 2

Reflex

Migration is a **reflex**. Birds react to changes in the seasons. Most birds in a single species leave at the same time. They head to the same place.

Learn more here!

Even caged birds have this reflex. They appear to want to migrate at the right time of year. The birds face the direction they would fly. They move around more than usual.

Chapter 3

Food

One reason for migration is hunger. In the north, some birds go hungry in the fall. There are fewer insects. Birds fly south in search of food. Many go to the **tropics**.

Learn more here!

By springtime, the tropics are crowded. There are more insects in the north. Birds fly north to eat.

Birds eat a lot of food to prepare for their long trips.

Birds may not migrate if there is enough food. They can ignore the reflex. If they do fly, they follow one of several **flyways**.

Bird feeders may help birds decide to stay up north.

Four Common Flight Paths

Chapter 4

Nesting

Birds also migrate to find good places for their nests. During northern winters, plants die or are covered in snow. Birds fly south where there are more plants.

Complete an activity here!

Plants grow during the spring. There are many places for birds to build nests. Birds fly north to **breed**.

Making Connections

Text-to-Self

Have you ever seen birds flying in a group together? What did you think they were doing?

Text-to-Text

Have you read other books about birds? What new thing did you learn?

Text-to-World

What might happen if birds stopped migrating?

Glossary

breed – to make babies.

flyway – a route often used by migrating birds.

migrate – to move from one area to another at a certain time.

reflex – an automatic response of the body in reaction to something.

species – a group of animals of the same kind that can have babies together.

tropics – the warm area surrounding the middle of the globe.

Index

Online Resources

popbooksonline.com

Thanks for reading this Cody Koala book!

Scan this code* and others like it in this book, or visit the website below to make this book pop!

popbooksonline.com/birds-fly-south

*Scanning QR codes requires a web-enabled smart device with a QR code reader app and a camera.